The Everyday Patriot

How To Be
A Great American
Now

Tom Morris

A Call To Action For Our Time

A Morris Institute Book

Graphic design by Dennis Walsak
Modular Graphics & Media, Wilmington, N.C.

Printed on International Paper's Beckett Concept acid free papers

"We have too many high sounding words,
and too few actions that correspond to them."

Abigail Adams (1744-1818)

To the everyday patriots
who live all around us.

Introduction

In The United States of America, we are citizens of the greatest nation in the history of the world, and yet, oddly, we've long been in danger of losing our grip on what citizenship means. To most of us these days, the idea of citizenship is little more than an abstraction. We pay our taxes, use the Postal Service to mail our letters, and perhaps watch a few fireworks on the Fourth of July. We may feel an inner stirring on hearing "America The Beautiful," the National Anthem, or "God Bless America." We might even have an American flag bumper sticker on the family car. But we don't typically walk around thinking of ourselves as Americans in any robust and important sense as we go through our normal routines.

★ ★ ★ ★ ★

Man was not born for himself alone, but for his country.
Plato

★ ★ ★ ★ ★

We do think of ourselves as belonging to a particular family, working at a specific place, pursuing a particular profession, and being part of a certain circle of friends. We may even feel a sense of identity or solidarity in connection with our neighborhood, our city, or even our state - but not like people once did. We've lost a sense of connection. And when it comes to the country as a whole, our basic citizenship is often at the outer periphery of our hearts and minds.

On September 11, 2001, something happened that shook us to the core and changed us all - but not nearly enough. In the aftermath of that tragic event, I've noticed the early signs of a renewal throughout the land, a resurgence of national spirit and pride. I bet you've felt it, too. It's bubbling up in fits and starts, but something is definitely at hand. Our hearts have been touched, and we're hoping for more. But there hasn't been enough real change as a result. We genuinely want something more for our country and for our own sense of ourselves as Americans, but we haven't done all we can to make things different. I think we're ready now.

* * * * *

Know your opportunity.
Pittacus

* * * * *

I want to encourage you to participate in this patriotic renewal, and to do so thoughtfully and intelligently, with a deep understanding of everything that's on the line, since we now stand at a crossroads in history. As Americans, we can be a shining example, or merely an object lesson, to all the rest of the world. I'm hoping we can come alive with a new enthusiasm for our potential role in the progress of humanity and get busy with the everyday patriotism that can make a huge positive difference for us all. That's what I want this little book to help you accomplish. I hope to persuade you, or at least to remind you, that great patriotism isn't just the province of those powerful individuals who steer the ship of state, and it isn't merely the business of those incredibly brave heroes whose actions inspire the nation. It's meant to be an important and fulfilling task for all of us throughout our lives.

★ ★ ★ ★ ★

Our country is the common parent of all.
Cicero

★ ★ ★ ★ ★

There was once a strong spirit in America. People felt connected with their communities and their country. We had tremendous pride in our cities, states, and nation. When I was growing up in the fifties and sixties, I was taught to sing, "I'm a Tar Heel Born, and a Tar Heel Bred, and when I Die I'll be Tar Heel Dead." I deeply identified with my immediate family, my house, my street, my hometown of Durham, and even the broader reaches of North Carolina. Our neighborhood was my playground. The Durham Bulls were my baseball team. I was a Carolina basketball fan. And I was a proud American. So were my friends. But as the years have passed, I've noticed a change.

We live in a highly mobile society. People feel less of a sense of place. We typically have less attachment to our state of residence, which may change every few years as we move from one job to another. We feel a diminished sense of community in our neighborhoods and cities. And at the same time, we've become so busy in our pursuits of love, and acceptance, and success that the overall realities of citizenship have also waned in our lives.

While the idea of citizenship has become a thin abstraction for so many Americans now, the more exalted idea of patriotism has grown a bit hollow in the eyes of many as well. It's at once still stubbornly attractive and yet somehow almost quaint. It can easily come across nowadays as an old-fashioned idea, a nostalgic holdover from the eras of Paul Revere and Pearl Harbor. But I've come to believe that a proper form of patriotism is one of the most important things in the world.

In this short book, I want to make a statement about citizenship and patriotism in our day. I'll lay out what it means for any of us to be patriotic citizens in all the best ways and then urge you to launch into a personal plan of action as a result. I want to help you think about what it takes not just to be an American, but to be a great American now.

★ ★ ★ ★ ★

Pursue worthy aims.
Solon

★ ★ ★ ★ ★

The ancient philosopher Plato believed that for any republic to prosper, every citizen in the land must play a proper role. Aristotle later declared that, "A city is a partnership for living well." I think his insight applies at every level. A neighborhood is a partnership for living well and so is a nation. We are all partners in a grand and vital enterprise. If we can come to understand that partnership more deeply, each of us can make the contribution we're here to make.

I once enjoyed reading a business book with the interesting title, *Perfecting a Piece of the World*. The everyday patriot is not often called upon to exhibit extraordinary courage or to accomplish anything of historical significance. The everyday patriot is just a person who works on a regular basis at improving his or her little piece of this nation, and thus on perfecting a piece of the world. It's all about choice. It's all about action. Let's look at what it takes. Then we can get going.

★ ★ ★ ★ ★

Action is the proper fruit of knowledge.
Thomas Fuller

★ ★ ★ ★ ★

★ ★ ★ ★ ★

Most people live, whether physically, intellectually
or morally, in a very restricted circle of their potential being.
They make use of a very small portion of their possible
consciousness, and of their soul's resources in general,
much like a man who, out of his whole bodily organism,
should get into a habit of using and moving only his little finger.
Great emergencies and crises show us how much greater
our vital resources are than we had supposed.

William James

★ ★ ★ ★ ★

How to Be a Great American

My fellow Americans (you wouldn't believe how much I've always wanted to say that): What would you come up with if I asked you right now to take out a piece of paper and make a list of great Americans? Whose names would immediately leap to mind? George Washington, Abraham Lincoln, Ben Franklin, Thomas Jefferson, Betsy Ross, Susan B. Anthony, Harry Truman, John Kennedy, Martin Luther King, Jr.? Most people would come up with a list that at least started with names like these. But notice something right away - It's a list of people in the past, people no longer alive.

★ ★ ★ ★ ★

He is great who confers the most benefits.
Emerson

★ ★ ★ ★ ★

Where are the great Americans now, the great Americans of the present day? I personally think they're all over the place. They're in New York City fire houses, police stations in Chicago, classrooms in Detroit. They're working the docks in San Francisco, staffing a senior center in Denver, volunteering at a hospital in Tulsa, commuting to work every day in Minneapolis, building a new business in Dallas. Some of them are plowing fields near Nashville, sitting on the city council in Phoenix, helping the Boys and Girls Club of Wilmington, and reading books to children right now in Miami, Cleveland, South Bend, and Charleston.

Actually, I think at least part of the answer to my question of where the great Americans are right now could possibly be that there are some in unexpected places in your own town, your neighborhood, and perhaps even your own home. You yourself may one day get onto someone's list.

I can imagine you might greet this particular speculation with a measure of skepticism. But maybe you shouldn't. After all, George Washington didn't begin life as a great American. He was once just a little boy in Virginia. Abraham Lincoln was a poor kid in the Midwest. Nobody could look at the little baby named Martin Luther King Jr. and tell that he would change the land. None of these individuals started life as great Americans. They became great because of the choices they made and what they did as a result, because of their determination to make a difference and all the actions for good that arose from that decision.

★ ★ ★ ★ ★

The loftiest towers rise from the ground.
Chinese proverb

★ ★ ★ ★ ★

It's been like that through the whole sweep of human history. In ancient times, even Alexander the Great had to start somewhere. When he was thirteen years old, he was just Alexander the Average - but he became great through what he learned and what he chose to do. That's the way it's been for all the great Americans in our national history as well. They started out just like you and I did.

They learned from those who had gone before them. And at some point they decided, as individuals, to take action and make a difference, if even in little ways. But as their examples show, when you do the little things right, you can end up having great results.

The Greatness that Counts

You don't have to get your picture into the history books to be a great American. You don't have to strut across a global stage, leading the nation, rousing the multitudes, and making the news. It's not necessary to be famous, or rich, or powerful. And you don't have to be a world-class hero either. You just have to decide, as an individual, to take action and make a difference for the good of others as well as yourself. Give something to your country. Give something to your community. Do something for your neighbors. Use your talents. Offer your time. Make your particular personal contribution for good.

★ ★ ★ ★ ★

To be an American is of itself almost
a moral condition, an education, and a career.
George Santayana

★ ★ ★ ★ ★

I want my life to make a difference. I bet you do, too. That's why we're here. We're born not just to take up space, wander through life and then die. We're in this world because we each have something to offer, something that in its own way can be great.

I'm a philosopher, believe it or not. I'm the first person in my family ever to go to college at all, and then I went on to graduate school. We couldn't afford it, but we somehow made it work, at the University of North Carolina for the first degree, and then on to Yale for a Ph.D. I taught at Notre Dame for fifteen years, and then gradually I began to hear a call to serve this country in a new way: to travel the nation as a public philosopher, talking with people about what all the great thinkers have had to say on the issues of success and happiness in life. One thing I've learned in the process is that personal success should never be measured in dollars or in power, in celebrity or in status. It's too often judged in precisely these terms, but that confuses the occasional trappings of success with what is really its heart. True success is a matter of the positive impact we have on other people, our individual contribution for good. It's the positive difference we make, each in our own way.

* * * * *

We cannot insure success, but we can deserve it.
John Adams

* * * * *

My parents were great Americans. They weren't rich or famous or powerful, but they were deeply successful: they made a difference for good. My mother was Rosie the Riveter in World War Two, at Martin Aircraft in Baltimore, up on a platform, holding a rivet gun, attaching the center section metal to the planes. She worked hard, and wouldn't let anyone else get away with shoddy results. She'd say, "Our boys' lives depend on this plane! Do it right or don't do it at all!" She was a great American.

My father was just off the farm, in his late teens and twenties, helping to design and build those planes. His boss told the War Department he knew as much about aircraft design at the age of twenty as anyone else in America. But the government said no twenty-year old could possibly know that much, so he ended up carrying a rifle in the South Pacific, serving this country any way he could. He lost his innocence, his best friend and his innate inner peace, but he never lost his determination to make a difference for his nation. I've seen him go to extraordinary lengths to help people newly arrived on our shores get off to the right start and live the American dream with their families. I believe my dad was a great American, too.

★ ★ ★ ★ ★

Great lives never go out. They go on.
Benjamin Harrison

★ ★ ★ ★ ★

Many of us can say the same thing about our parents or grandparents, and older aunts and uncles. They served this country well. They believed in our nation. They lived its values day to day. They made sacrifices. They took action. They helped their neighbors. They made a difference.

I'm glad we can say that about so many of those who've come before us. But here's the question for us today: Are our kids going to be able to say the same thing about us? Will they one day come to think of us as the great Americans in our time? We can give them something to be proud of, too, but only if we take the right sort of action and make the real difference with our lives we're capable of making.

* * * * *

In the arena of human life, the honors and rewards
fall to those who show their good qualities in action.
Aristotle

* * * * *

And that's the problem. We've long known there are three kinds of people in the world: those who make things happen, those who watch things happen, and those who go around saying, "What happened?" Too many of us have fallen into the wrong category. Life isn't a spectator sport, and neither is patriotism. Citizenship isn't meant to be a passive state of mind. You don't serve your country by just doing your job, minding your business and biding your time. You have to get off the bench and get into the game. You're needed. I'm needed. If we can figure out how to take action with our lives for the sake of our country - if only in little ways, day to day - we can make a positive difference for a long time to come.

Let me put it another way: America is a great garden of possibilities. Don't be a weed! Don't even be a prize petunia. Be one of the active gardeners of our time! And then why not be a great one? What's the patriotic equivalent of a green thumb? Have a red, white and blue thumb, and show it in your life day to day. We all need to get busy and tend the garden we've been given, now.

All gardeners live in beautiful places because they make them so.
Joseph Joubert

Real Patriotism

For the first time ever (I have to admit I'm a little embarrassed to tell you I'd never done this before), I hung an American flag outside my house on the Fourth of July this year. Actually, I put seventeen flags out there. "Why seventeen?" you may wonder. I guess I just ran out of room. But you know what? Planting flags in the garden alone won't do it. Putting bumper stickers on the car by itself isn't enough. I can wear red, white and blue every time I leave the house, but that won't get the job done either. I need to figure out how to use my particular talents and spend a little bit of my time to take some real action and make a difference for this country. It might just be some small new ways of getting more involved that could end up generating big results.

You need to figure out what you can do, too. The symbols of patriotism are great. They're ours to use with pride. But the time has come when we need the real thing as well. And that means we need a little dedicated action.

The test of any man lies in action.
Pindar

Here's the problem. We get action only through motivation. But for a long time in America, we've lacked motivation for a full, robust, active sense of patriotic citizenship. The book of Proverbs in the Bible says, "Without a vision, the people perish." We've been without a vision for far too long—Most of us have had no big, positive vision for our lives, our families, our neighborhoods, our towns, and our nation. And people have perished as a result. Only a powerful, positive vision for what being an American really means can possibly motivate us to take the sort of action we need in order to make the right kind of difference in our time.

I grew up with a strongly positive view of this country and its potential. I've always been proud to be an American, and as a child felt like I was a part of a big extended national family that embraced me as an individual. In those years, I even imagined that I was somehow directly connected to our government, that it was in some personal sense mine and that our national leaders were really concerned about me. When President John F. Kennedy was in office and I was a student in elementary school, I occasionally lay on the floor of our small four-room house and drew cartoons for the president's children, Caroline and John-John. One day, I put a few of those sketches into an envelope and addressed it to The White House, Washington, DC. My parents stuck on some stamps and dropped it into the mailbox. Weeks later, a beautiful, crisp white envelope arrived by return mail. In the upper left corner, in raised blue ink, it said "The White House." I remember holding it in my hands and feeling very important, but not at all surprised. I opened it carefully and read a nice note from Mrs. Kennedy's personal assistant, thanking me for the drawings and telling me how much Caroline and John-John had enjoyed them. In America, I was convinced, every child counts. Each one of us is genuinely important to our nation.

★★★★★

Every man feels instinctively that all the beautiful sentiments
In the world weigh less than a single lovely action.
J.R. Lowell

★★★★★

A few years later, at the age of twelve, I engaged in a classroom debate about one man's national political aims as if our little discussion would have an impact on the upcoming election. In graduate school, I went door to door campaigning for a presidential candidate in the middle of the most hostile territory he faced in the country. It mattered that much to me. And I credited the outcome of that election, at least in small part, to the cosmic impact of my doorstep orations.

From a young age, I had at least a basic understanding of patriotism. In later life, as a philosopher, I've learned that wisdom is all about perspective and context, framing our experiences properly, seeing things in the right light and appreciating the real connections events have to each other. Patriotism begins with matters of perspective and context, too. It means thinking in a broader horizon and seeing beyond our usual personal concerns. It involves having a bigger picture for our lives than a simple, near-sighted selfishness and it means acting for the sake of a greater good - a good that eventually and wonderfully will redound to the best long-term self-interest of us all. I certainly hadn't thought through any of this intellectually as a child or adolescent, but since my early years, I had at least an incipient understanding of it all.

★ ★ ★ ★ ★

We have advanced far enough to say that democracy is a way of life. We have yet to realize that it is a way of personal life and one which provides a moral standard for personal conduct.
John Dewey

★ ★ ★ ★ ★

I'm sharing with you this small bit of my background in patriotic thought and action not because I've had any real hand in the political fortunes of our country at all, but just to show how much of an American I grew up feeling myself to be, and how naturally connected I felt, in ways important to me, with the bigger picture of our national governance and electoral process. And yet, even so, it wasn't long before marriage, career, fatherhood, work and just the general busyness of adult life had displaced my sense of citizenship almost entirely. As an adult, I was capable of benefiting from, and contributing to, our national life in many more ways than I had as a child and even as a student. But somehow, the thrill was gone. I began taking for granted the ebb and flow of daily life, all that's convenient in this country, all that's available, and all that's possible because of our unique laws, structures and freedoms. I lost my motivation to engage in acts of patriotic service at any level. I didn't debate the issues of the day. I didn't join any other political campaigns. I didn't even draw any more cartoons for presidential kids.

* * * * *

The death of democracy is not likely to be an assassination from ambush. It will be a slow extinction from apathy, indifference, and undernourishment.
Robert Hutchins

* * * * *

Hitting Bottom

My patriotism bottomed out. In fact, like a lot of people, I came to think of patriotism as basically good-hearted and old-fashioned, but in the current age a little over the top, like that aggressive school spirit manifested by cheering too loudly for your high school team when you were already up by thirty points against an obviously weaker opponent. There was even something a little awkward and almost embarrassing about overt displays of nationalistic pride. I lost touch with politics. I took a more casual attitude toward the news. And in very little time, I drifted into what I can only describe in retrospect as feeling almost completely unconnected from my community. My little world had shrunk that far. I'm a little ashamed to admit that in one election I can remember, I didn't even go to the trouble of voting. It was just a local election, I didn't know that much about any of the candidates, and on election day I was at first too busy and then, as a result, too tired to go and vote.

★ ★ ★ ★ ★

I find excuses for myself.
Horace

★ ★ ★ ★ ★

Too tired to vote. Can you imagine that? Or do you know the feeling first hand? How can anyone be too tired to vote? I can understand being too tired to play another nine holes of golf after completing eighteen, feeling too tired to finish mowing the grass on a really hot day, being too tired for a pickup game of basketball after a long stretch at work, or feeling too tired to go out dancing late at night. But, too tired to vote? Check your name off here, then walk over there, duck behind that curtain - Click, click, click, pull. Too tired for that?

I wasn't really too tired. I was just unmotivated. I had lost my sense of the importance of citizenship and its activities. I didn't vote because somewhere deep in my heart I was thinking, "Why bother? What difference does it make?"

We have so many excuses for not exercising our democratic right to vote. But this is a right that people in other parts of the world have longed for and struggled mightily to attain. It's a right that people in our own country have fought and died to secure. In fact, there are far too many young men and women who continue to have to suffer and die to protect it. And we stay home with excuses. Just think for a second about all the utterly unoriginal things we sometimes say to rationalize our inertia: "My one vote won't make any difference." "The candidates are all alike – what's the choice?" "My loving spouse will vote the other way and cancel mine out. So we both just stay home and call it even." Then there is the apparently sensitive, caring, distracted slacker claim: "I don't know the candidates well enough to make an informed decision. I'd do more harm than good by voting this time around."

★ ★ ★ ★ ★

In the conduct of life we make use of deliberation
to justify ourselves in doing what we want to do.
W. Somerset Maugham

★ ★ ★ ★ ★

Every vote sends a message, whether it counts as the margin of victory or not. And if no two people are exactly alike, no two candidates are, either. We always have a choice. When any two people who disagree on politics stay home to keep from canceling each other out, their absence from the process sends a vote of "no confidence" all by itself. It says, "This isn't worth the trouble of going down the street." It's an insult to the sacrifices made by good men and women for over two hundred years, and it subtly erodes the foundations of future freedom and democracy in America, as well as throughout the world. It's never without a point to go and cast a vote.

★ ★ ★ ★ ★

At the bottom of all the tributes paid to democracy is the little man, walking into the little booth, with a little pencil, making a little cross on a little bit of paper – no amount of rhetoric or voluminous discussion can possibly diminish the overwhelming importance of this point.
Winston Churchill

★ ★ ★ ★ ★

The ignorance excuse for not voting, if it's sincere, is a real problem indeed. But there are, in principle, two ways of dealing with any problem. Problems can be solved or, better yet, avoided. If election day rolls around, and you suddenly realize you know nothing about the candidates on the ballot, you do have a problem. And it's a problem the rest of us share, because an ignorant or frivolous vote can hurt us all, in however small a way. I suppose the person who lacks electoral knowledge could solve his problem on the spot to some extent by casting a straight party ballot, and just align himself with the basic approach to government he feels best about, trusting the party leadership to have made an informed decision for him. That would be better than not voting at all, but admittedly not by a lot. The obvious disadvantages of relying on that simple approach cry out for a strategy of problem avoidance instead. Even an hour or two on the internet can provide lots of information for the otherwise clueless voter. We should anticipate any election and get as informed on the issues and candidates as we can. It's not that hard.

* * * * *

The ignorance of one voter in a democracy
impairs the security of all.
John F. Kennedy

* * * * *

I am convinced that, ultimately, all the excuses we give for not participating more in the democratic process, for not giving more to our communities with our time and talents, and for not caring much about anything beyond the ends of our own noses are really nothing more than mere smokescreens around a basic lack of motivation. We have no vision. We have no sense of ourselves as citizens. We have no enthusiasm for, or emotional commitment to, the underlying conditions that make possible the freedom we so enjoy. And that's a problem worth solving.

Most people seem to think that citizenship is just a matter of fact and patriotism is a matter of feeling - as if your citizenship is merely a legal fact about where you were born or where you've sought and attained the requisite official status, and patriotism is a completely separate issue about emotions, or feelings of loyalty and pride. Citizenship is really all about duty, responsibility and privilege. It's a moral status, not just a political fact, and it's meant to be a matter of personal commitment as well. Patriotism is a deeply related matter of belief, feeling and motivated action from the heart, in support of the nation in which you are a citizen. Where motivation is low, patriotism languishes, and citizenship suffers along with it. Without the proper motivational support, none of us will do what we ought.

★ ★ ★ ★ ★

When you cease to make a contribution, you begin to die.
Eleanor Roosevelt

★ ★ ★ ★ ★

I recently read something that quickly made a huge motivational difference in my own life. Actually, it's something that's made a very big difference for all of us, whether we're aware of it or not: our national birth certificate, the Declaration of Independence. One of the greatest documents in all of human history, this short proclamation launched our nation into its place in the world over two hundred years ago. Reading it recently, really reading it carefully and thinking hard about everything it says, has reignited my sense of what this country stands for. It has re-established my understanding of what authentic patriotism is, and has renewed my personal vision for what we can all do now to join the ranks of great Americans throughout the years.

The Declaration of Our Independence

You remember reading the Declaration of Independence in school a long time ago, I bet. "Four score and seven years ago" – no, of course I'm kidding. That's the beginning of Abraham Lincoln's famous Gettysburg Address. The Declaration of Independence starts with the words, "When in the course of human events". Let's look at the whole opening statement of that great document.

> *When in the course of human events it becomes necessary for one people to dissolve the political bands which have connected them with another, and to assume among the powers of the earth the separate and equal station to which the laws of nature and of nature's God entitle them, a decent respect to the opinions of mankind requires that they should declare the causes which impel them to the separation.*

Our predecessors on the scene in that summer of 1776 decided it was time to declare our independence as a nation, to separate ourselves apart from other sovereign national entities, and to take our rightful standing in the world as a unified people.

They also thought it would be appropriate to explain to the rest of the world what we were doing and why. To accomplish that task, they created and approved this great document, a profound statement of purpose that should continue to be a guiding light for every American in each generation. I was fifty years old before I rediscovered it and realized its ongoing importance for my life, as well as for the rest of us.

★ ★ ★ ★ ★

If the American Revolution had produced nothing
but the Declaration of Independence,
it would have been worth while.
Samuel Eliot Morrison

★ ★ ★ ★ ★

On that auspicious day of July 4, 1776, when the final draft of this document was read and approved by our representatives in the Second Continental Congress, two hundred large "broadsides" of the Declaration were printed in Philadelphia, to be taken throughout the thirteen original colonies so they could be read and viewed in public places. Only twenty-five of these two hundred still exist. Twenty-four are protected in museums or otherwise locked up, but the twenty-fifth was discovered just a short time ago, bought at auction, and sent out on a road trip around America so that citizens like you and me, who might not have easy access to a great museum or library, could see and read in person one of those original historical proclamations of our national birth.

When I began reading it for the first time as an adult, it didn't take me long to get excited about what I was seeing. Sentence two grabbed me right away:

> *We hold these truths to be self evident, that all men are created equal, that they are endowed by their creator with certain unalienable rights, that among these are life, liberty and the pursuit of happiness.*

With these words, the greatest democracy in the world was launched – the land of the free and the home of the brave. With these simple, powerful claims and those that followed, it was announced that a new nation is on the map, a country whose point of existence is to acknowledge the value and fundamental rights of every human being, and to offer us all the chance to create our own futures - a nation from its founding committed to giving each of us the opportunity to grow, prosper and be happy, the chance to have loving families, great neighborhoods and good work – an invitation to make a positive difference with our lives.

★ ★ ★ ★ ★

America means opportunity, freedom, power.
Emerson

★ ★ ★ ★ ★

Consider the claim that all men are created equal. We're certainly not all born equal in size, social status or talent. We can't sing equally well or speak with equal fluency, throw a ball with equal power, dance with equal grace or swing a golf club with equal effect. We can't spell equally well, or calculate with equal agility. We clearly differ in so many ways. The Declaration of Independence doesn't deny any of this at all. It just reminds us that we are born with equal human value, and equal basic rights that deserve to be respected. We are equal under the law, equally worthy of legal protection and equally deserving of the opportunity to grow, prosper and be happy. We're equally innocent until proved guilty, equally worthy of having a voice and equally powerful with that voice whenever we vote. We're all equally deserving of a chance to make a difference.

Thomas Jefferson initially drafted the words that we read in the Declaration of Independence to express what a great many people within these shores had already come to believe in 1776. We needed a new nation dedicated to these principles. We needed a special place on God's earth to try them out, put them into practice and then share what we learned, as a result, with the world. No other nation was conceived and created for such a reason. We are unique.

★ ★ ★ ★ ★

The preservation of the sacred fire of liberty,
and the destiny of the republican model of government,
is justly considered as deeply,
perhaps as finally staked, on the experiment entrusted
to the hands of the American people.
George Washington

★ ★ ★ ★ ★

Life, Liberty, and the Greatest Pursuit

"Life, liberty, and the pursuit of happiness." Life is a gift. Liberty is an achievement. The pursuit of happiness is an ongoing process essential to the human condition. Any gift can be taken away, any achievement can be lost and any process of great importance can be blocked by forces arrayed against it. Such forces can imperil liberty and threaten life as well. To secure any of these basic rights and to protect their exercise, we need to be vigilant and engaged in their defense in a great many ways.

★ ★ ★ ★ ★

Americanism consists in utterly believing
in the principles of America.
Woodrow Wilson

★ ★ ★ ★ ★

We can appreciate the values behind our nation only when we properly understand that the happiness the founders insisted we are free to pursue is not a fragile or passing state of mind. It's not just a feeling of pleasure or a temporary sense of satisfaction. Happiness is a fundamental state of being. It's the factual, objective reality of personal fulfillment, a by-product of growth and learning and good work. This is something genuinely happy people seem to understand. Happiness consists in exercising our talents, flourishing as individuals and enjoying great relationships with others. It is the pinnacle of human existence, and according to many ancient thinkers, the purpose of our being as well.

* * * * *

We may define happiness as prosperity combined with virtue.
Aristotle

* * * * *

In my work as a public philosopher over the past decade, I've come to realize that true success in life or work is never just an individual accomplishment, and neither is real happiness. The highest and deepest forms of success and happiness are always made possible by our liberty – our freedom - and by the opportunities our great nation provides for us to work with other people, using our hearts and minds and hands to do good in the world. That's the way it is in life. Where you live can determine what you can do and who you can become. Your social and political circumstances can allow your dreams to come true, or keep you from even having a chance. The best possible surroundings can magnify your shot at success in everything you do. That's just what our great country was designed to provide. Despite our flaws and imperfections, we've got the basics right. They're the fundamental values behind our Declaration of Independence. We can make this country and our lives increasingly better if we'll just live these values every day.

He loves his country best who tries to make it best.
R. W. Ingersoll

A little kid in our land can grow up to be a hero - a healer, a teacher, a great athlete, a world leader, a role model to millions - or simply a good person: a friend, a mother or dad, and a kind, helpful neighbor. Everything is possible to us here. We can dream and do and succeed like no one else on earth, thanks to the extensive freedoms we enjoy as Americans.

Real American patriotism understands this. It works to secure and enhance and consistently embody the values that make this liberty, and this life of ours, possible. Genuine patriotism isn't just a state of mind or a warm fuzzy feeling. It's not merely an attitude of approval and support. It's an inner determination to act, together with an outer pattern of action that delivers real good into the world. It's a positive involvement in the life of our nation, on however small or large a scale. It's supportive and creative. It isn't inherently exclusionary at all.

★ ★ ★ ★ ★

I venture to suggest that patriotism is not a short and frenzied outburst of emotion but the tranquil and steady dedication of a lifetime.
Adlai E. Stevenson

★ ★ ★ ★ ★

A full-bodied sense of affiliation, combined with a strong noble loyalty, doesn't have to involve any exclusivity of concern. Stronger families make stronger communities; stronger communities can make for a stronger nation; and stronger nations can join to create a better world. This is what I like to call the "Inner Circle Principle." Building good relations in our innermost circles of family, friends, and neighbors can form the basis for building better relations on a broader scale as well, moving outward from where we start. A broadest possible concern for the world does not require any lack of concern for home, or a less than enthusiastic embracing of our own heritage and land. A Frenchman can love France without denigrating everyone else, however hard that might be to believe these days. An American can love our nation for the sake of the rest of the world.

The best American patriotism is invitational. It isn't jingoistic, xenophobic, inherently prejudiced or tribal, a dichotomized "us against them." It's based on the deepest values that ultimately can unite rather than divide. It's a readiness to put these values into action and celebrate their importance for a life of significance.

What are those values? There are many, but seven stand at the core: Life, Liberty, Equality, Opportunity, Justice, Security, and Service. Americans celebrate life. At our best, we value and protect it wherever we can. We seek to enrich and preserve it, and help make it worth living. At least, we do this when we are consistently living the core of our founding vision.

*****

The care of human life and happiness, and not their destruction,
is the first and only legitimate object of government.
Thomas Jefferson

*****

In the eyes of the world, America at its best stands for liberty – the freedom of people to respond to this world with the best that is within them, the freedom to discover their talents, develop those talents and deploy them into the world for the good of others as well as themselves. This liberty represented by our nation is the freedom to learn and grow and flourish, as well as to be involved in choosing those social rules under which we all shall live. We too often exercise our liberty as if it were no more than license. The core of freedom is not permissive, irresponsible indulgence, and most of us know that well. But we need to live more consistently with what we understand. Freedom from oppression and undue restraint is freedom for a purpose – and the nobility of purpose we choose is what gives our freedom its worth.

*****

Freedom has its life in the heart, the actions, the spirit of men,
and so it must be daily earned and refreshed – else like a flower
cut from its life giving roots, it will wither and die.
Dwight D. Eisenhower

*****

America also aims at the fundamental value of equality. It was founded to recognize, respect and defend the basic equality of all human beings that lies beneath our great and numerous differences. This is a value we have struggled to live consistently, and have come better to approximate only with the many passing decades since our founding. It's our commitment, our hope and the strength of our future.

The value of equality is tied up with that of opportunity. Equality has to do with more than fair treatment under the law. In America, we believe that every human being should have, in as strong a sense as we can possibly provide, an equal opportunity for personal development and success. Again, this is often more an aspiration than a reality in the lives of too many of our citizens, but a dream and a driving hope it is indeed. We are committed by the philosophy of our founding to its importance.

Justice is an American value. The main body of the Declaration of Independence details the injustices that led us as a people to break away and constitute ourselves as a sovereign nation, in pursuit of that justice we had not otherwise been able to find. Here again, this is not something we claim to have attained in any degree remotely close to perfection, but it is something to which we, as Americans, are committed, and to which we must fervently aspire.

★ ★ ★ ★ ★

Justice is truth in action.
Joseph Joubert

★ ★ ★ ★ ★

Security is the condition needed in order for life to be sustained, liberty to flourish, equality to be respected, opportunity to be provided and justice to prevail. It is only under these conditions that a full and enlightened pursuit of happiness for each of us, and those we love, is possible.

★ ★ ★ ★ ★

The only liberty I mean, is a liberty connected with order;
that not only exists along with order and virtue,
but which cannot exist at all without them.
Edmund Burke

★ ★ ★ ★ ★

Considering together this array of national values can help us appreciate their inter-connections. A measure of security is needed for the sustenance of life, as well as for its full enjoyment. Any process or apparatus of security that needlessly endangers or diminishes life would be inconsistent with that other important value for the sake of which it exists.

In a parallel way, our concern for national security is meant to protect our liberty, not subvert it. Conversely, our understanding of liberty must be compatible with the need for that security. Each must coordinate with the other. This is true of all our basic, founding American values. Any one of them must be understood, developed and implemented in a manner consistent with all the others. The whole cluster of founding values underlying the Declaration of Independence together constitutes the basis for the great American dream.

At the heart of everyday patriotism is the value of service - service to our family members, our neighbors, our friends, our communities, and our nation. This founding American value is meant to extend ultimately into a service to our world. We owe other people our lives. Others brought us into this world, provided us with a context in which we could grow and be free, and ask nothing more in return than that we keep this in mind as we make our choices day to day.

We have been well served by many of those who came before us. It is our duty and great privilege to return the favor and act in service to people now living and still others yet to be born. Our government on every level exists for the purpose of serving us all, and never just an elite few. It is for this service that we give it our consent and our allegiance.

A Message to the World

As we've all recently learned in an unforgettable way there are people in this world who misunderstand our values, fear our freedoms, and hope to bring them all to an end. They desperately want our great experiment in democracy to fail. They've killed thousands of us. They'd prefer millions. They've already left far too many little boys and girls without parents, husbands without wives, moms without dads and friends with huge gaping holes in their lives. But they haven't left the rest of us without options. I believe we need to send them a message today, tomorrow and the day after that.

We must meet our duty and convince the world that we are just friends and brave enemies.
Thomas Jefferson

We will not be terrorized into quitting. We will not be cowed by misunderstandings, mistaken hatreds, or misplaced violence. We will continue. We will improve. And we will prevail. America certainly isn't a perfect place – we all know that - but in a great many ways, it's the best place there is, and we can all take action to make it even better. This is a place where almost anything is possible. This is a land where initiative, persistence, creativity and love can conquer hate, overcome misunderstanding, correct mistakes and build something new, noble and of great lasting value.

We need to send a signal to the world. We need to get a message out to the whole globe that we believe in this nation, that we are committed to its health and that we intend to stand by it - to stand by each other - in tough times as well as in good times. We can't do that by just flying the flag or wearing a USA T-shirt. We can't make our point with merely the symbols of patriotism, great as they are. We need to show the world the real thing, now.

You can't prove you're an American by waving Old Glory.
Helen Gahagan Douglas

How can we send out a message like that? What can we do to show the whole world the way we really feel? Well, for one thing, we can exercise our distinctively democratic right and vote.

Vote in the next election. Vote in every election. Vote even when there is no election! Vote with your attention, your conversation, and your energies, day to day. Read the papers, keep up on the news, get involved in your community, take action, do something good, and make your views known.

*To make democracy work, we must be a nation
of participants, not simply observers.*
Louis L'Amour

When I get worked up about an issue, and think my voice should be heard, I write my congressional representative or senator. Maybe you've done this too. I know, I know: we get these form letters back. "Dear Constituent" - and that can be a bit disheartening. But don't be discouraged. Even if you want to write them a form letter yourself, voice your views. One way or another, you will be heard.

Real democratic voting is not something that happens just on a special day set aside every couple of years. Real voting is something we do with our hands and feet, arms and legs and minds on a regular basis. It's going on all around us. I'm thinking of a young Ivy-league graduate who just left a job in New York to enlist in the marines. I know a consultant and trained historian now having the time of his life as a scoutmaster. An accomplished woman in town successfully organized the funding and construction of a beautiful new branch for the public library. Meanwhile, a retired business star votes with his time and energy every week to build up the local Boys and Girls Club, as well as many other community organizations that support those founding American values we hold so dear. These are people who vote every day. They are examples of the everyday patriots in our time. Let's join in their efforts and enjoy with them the great satisfaction that comes from doing the right thing for our nation whenever we can.

★ ★ ★ ★ ★

Action is eloquence.
Shakespeare

★ ★ ★ ★ ★

Doing unto others as we would have them do unto us – living out the American dream of life, liberty, equality, opportunity, justice, security and service every day, in our towns and neighborhoods, in our volunteer organizations, our churches and synagogues and mosques will do great good, and send out an important message. It won't be a message as easily quantifiable as voter turnout on election days, but it will be a message just as important for conveying our deep and genuine commitment to America, and through this nation, to the best aspirations of the world.

The everyday patriot in our land is committed in principle to the good of the world. The Declaration of Independence, after all, says that all men are created equal, not just those who live within our borders. This great claim applies to men and women in Afghanistan, Iraq, Iran, North Korea, Somalia, and any other country where little children have grown up without the most basic freedom and opportunity to become what they are capable of being. The values of our land are a beacon in the night for all who aspire to the best in this life. We're just trying to blaze the way, clear the path and provide real hope for the world. Our small patriotic actions each day can strengthen that hope for everyone.

No Time for Cynics

As a nation, we've joked about politics and politicians for a long time now. A few of our leaders have given us plenty to laugh at. But we don't have time to be cynical any longer. Not every politician is a crook. Not every lobbyist is a liar. Government employees aren't incompetent fools. There are good and bad people in every profession. There is reality and mere appearance in every walk of life. Politics is no different. And it's unavoidably important. The task of government is simply a necessity at every level of our lives. We all have to govern our selves, our households and our careers. To play on Plato, as he once quoted Socrates, the ungoverned life is not worth living. Politics is the human way of serving our needs of governance at every level. Aristotle once stated that "Man is a political animal," and he didn't intend by this to insult either us or the animals. At its best, politics is life – it's the life of people together, adjudicating their differences, working out their hopes and leaving their legacy to the future.

* * * * *

Cynics are only happy in making the world as barren
for others as they have made it for themselves.
George Meredith.

A cynical mindset about politics or life is a luxury we can no longer afford. We can still be properly skeptical about any particular person who enters the political arena; we can and should question any specific policy or program offered for our consideration; we can debate all issues of importance with feeling – it's our right and our duty. But we need to put our cynical disregard for politics and politicians behind us. For years, we've understood that health care isn't just the business of physicians and health care professionals. It's everybody's business. In the same way, we need to realize that politics isn't just the business of politicians. It's your business and mine.

This is our country. Let's reclaim it. Let's take our cue and our motivation from the Declaration of Independence. Let's declare our independence from apathy, noninvolvement, and inertia. Let's put aside our cynical disregard for the political process. Let's quit deriding politicians and dismissing their intentions. Let's raise the bar instead. By our positive attention and concern we can make a real change, and we should—not because it's our duty, but because it's our right. It's in our self-interest to take action now; to preserve, protect and enhance our democracy.

★ ★ ★ ★ ★

What we need are critical lovers of America – patriots
who express their faith in their country
by working to improve it.
Hubert H. Humphrey

★ ★ ★ ★ ★

I don't think the founders of this country worked and fought for our freedom to have desperate slums, polluted cities, murdered children, corporate theft, homeless families and shattered lives. They didn't yearn for a superficial throwaway culture where inner growth is sacrificed to outer comfort and basic necessities are destroyed by reckless behavior. They wanted us to be a light to the world, not a stumbling block, a source of hope, not a cause of hate. To the extent that we've diverged from their dreams, we have some serious work to do. And, when we think of all those who have given their time, talents and lives so that we might succeed in attaining those dreams, we should be inspired to get busy in that work. Let's do everything we can to see to it that no young nineteen-year-old patriot, eager to serve our country, has ever perished in vain. We can make those sacrifices count in our own day. It's up to each and every one of us.

For too many of us, for far too long, citizenship has been a diaphanous cape whose ethereal fabric we could barely see or feel. Or else it's been a rough wool shirt too uncomfortable to wear. Let's change that now. Let's make our American citizenship a positive, active reality in our lives. Let's show that patriotism is indeed much more than just flying the flag or singing the National Anthem or even pledging allegiance. Let's honor the founders of this nation and make them proud. Let's honor each other and make each other proud. Let's honor our children. Let's make them and their children proud.

The Great American Revival

Winston Churchill long ago said, "You can always depend on Americans to do the right thing, once they've exhausted every other possibility." All right, we'll take it. We've tried everything else. We've tried leaving the business of America to other people, and we've learned some important lessons. Now we're going to do the right thing, reawaken our attention and retake the concern that should never have left us in the first place. The business of America is indeed yours and mine.

The great end of life is not knowledge, but action.
T.H. Huxley

I feel a new spirit moving across the land. The worst we can experience has always brought out the best in us. The challenges from those who hate us, and the scandals of those who would exploit us, have issued a wakeup call for us all. This is a time for revival, a time to renew the true patriotic spirit in America. I see the first positive stirrings of a rebirth of national feeling, focused on the values that lie behind the Declaration of Independence, our American Constitution, the Gettysburg Address and all the great statements of national vision we have inherited from our past. I see my neighbors and friends wanting to take action and make a difference with their lives. And I see them beginning to do so in profound and practical ways.

I'm reminded of a letter the great American, Abigail Adams, wrote to her husband, John, while he was away from home, in Philadelphia during 1776, working hard to help create this country we enjoy and love. She wanted to encourage him to give his best to the enterprise. She had to remind him of the importance of the moment. To do so, she quoted some of her favorite lines in Shakespeare, a passage from the play "Julius Caesar" (Act 4, Scene iii) that reads, in full:

There is a tide in the affairs of men,
Which, taken at the flood, leads on to fortune;
Omitted, all the voyage of their life
Is bound in shallows and in miseries.
On such a full sea are we now afloat,
And we must take the current when it serves,
Or lose our ventures.

Let's take that current we have right now. Let's set out on that rising tide and sail on to our great destiny together. Let's take action and make the difference for each other, for America and for the world that we are here on this earth to make.

★ ★ ★ ★ ★

The conduct of our lives is the true mirror of our doctrine.
Montaigne

★ ★ ★ ★ ★

Vote every day. Show the world what you really think. Be a great American in your own personal way. Hug your kids. Read to them. Kiss your spouse. Show you care. Help a friend. Do something good for somebody. Check on a neighbor. Give blood. Pick up some litter. And when your next Jury Duty notice arrives, don't suddenly become the Houdini of public service. Go do it well. Use your heart, mind and will. You can start small in showing your everyday patriotism or in raising its level a notch, but do indeed start. Take action for this nation and make the difference that only you can make.

The Declaration of Independence ends with the words, "We

mutually pledge to each other our lives, our fortunes, and our sacred honor." Let's all of us make a mutual pledge in our own hearts to each other and to our nation, today and every day we live.

Our Line in the Sand

I've recently wondered, with more than a little frustration, why it has taken me fifty years on this earth to come to some of these simple realizations. I wonder also why it is that so many people who recently have described themselves to me as feeling a new sense of patriotism seem to be about my same age. It could be that there is a very basic explanation for this—at least, I think I have a guess.

There may be four stages of life in modern America, each one consisting of about twenty-five years, if we're blessed with good health and longevity. Each of these stages is defined by a focal activity – not by an activity unique to it, but by one that receives a particular emphasis within its boundaries. The first quarter century of our lives is focused on learning. We're busy learning about the world, other people and ourselves. Our initial educations and the subsequent training we receive in particular professions or vocations we'll pursue usually takes about this long, or longer.

★ ★ ★ ★ ★

It is no profit to have learned well, if you neglect to do well.
Publilius Syrus

★ ★ ★ ★ ★

The second stage of life centers on building. We're building families, careers, homes, mature relationships, skill sets, networks of friendships and our reputations in what we do. In this stage, we typically begin to define ourselves in terms of what we're building and in relation to those things we've already managed to create. This naturally becomes a primary source of identity for each of us.

The third stage of life then can, or at least should, be focused on serving. That's the stage I've finally hit in a big way. And that's why serving my fellow citizens and my nation has suddenly become so important to me. At a certain point, we have in our possession tools for service that have been developed for a fairly long time. We no longer need to concentrate so hard on using those tools to build our careers or businesses. The basic structures are in place. It's a natural time to turn our attention to serving others in as broad a way as we can.

And then there's the culminating stage four, from the ages of about seventy five to one hundred (and perhaps even beyond), in which guiding can become our main mission – guiding others with the accumulated wisdom we have attained through our failures and successes, our dreams and triumphs and the many observations we've made on the way. Great cultures derive guidance from those elders in their midst who have become sages as a result of their journeys and adventures. We never stop learning, building or serving if we are in fact wise. But this period of the journey can involve a new concentration on guiding those who come after us.

Some wisdom must be learned from one who is wise.
Euripides

Of course, none of these activities is exclusive to its respective stage in any sense at all. The best young people build skills and friendships that can be theirs for a lifetime, serve others while learning and give whatever guidance they can to their younger companions along the way. I was always so proud of my students while I taught at Notre Dame, for their volunteer work in the community as Big Brothers and Big Sisters and in so many other ways. These forms of service weren't just compatible with their educations - they were educations in themselves.

Likewise, young adults who are in their main life-building stage will never truly flourish if they don't continue to learn, and seek to serve their neighbors and communities in any way they're able. They can also be an important source of guidance to those who are not yet as far down life's road.

Service in the third stage can involve important forms of building, and is done best while learning new things in new ways that can deepen what we have to offer to the world. I see many third-stagers going back to the classics, reading the great books of the past, attending plays, and exploring new realms of art that enrich their lives.

Finally, our elder sages in stage four sometimes amaze me with their hunger for new knowledge, their desire to help launch new enterprises, and their commitment to serve. Every one of these activities should inform each of the stages of our lives, but we should not be at all surprised to see our priorities subtly shift as age carries us along to new vistas and new opportunities.

★ ★ ★ ★ ★

Every stage in human life, except the last, is marked out
by certain and defined limits; old age alone
has no precise and determinate boundary.
Cicero

★ ★ ★ ★ ★

In the founding years of our nation's life, Benjamin Franklin was a great example of a man flourishing in all these ways in all four stages. Born in 1706 as the fifteenth of seventeen children, he was largely self-educated in stage one and beyond. During his building years, he published the *Pennsylvania Gazette*, and *Poor Richard's Almanac*, while starting a fire department, becoming postmaster, founding the American Philosophical Society and using that famous kite for electrical research. His stage three service launched him into work for the Pennsylvania Assembly and involved extensive time in England where he tried hard to reconcile the colonies and the crown until the effort became futile. He then returned home to Philadelphia and helped shepherd the Continental Congress toward their Declaration of Independence.

His stage four guidance began quite early and culminated with his vital role in the creation of the American Constitution while he was in his early eighties.

★ ★ ★ ★ ★

Men are all alike in their promises.
It is only in their deeds that they differ.
Molière

★ ★ ★ ★ ★

It may have taken me half a century to get here, but as a philosopher and an American I'm thrilled to be at the stage of seeking new ways to serve my neighbors, my country and my world. I've begun right off to learn new and exciting things about the history of this country, I've started building up new ideas and new structures for the delivery of my distinctive form of service, and I now look forward to the time when I can give even more valuable guidance than I now can supply for the greater success, fulfillment and happiness of everyone around me. I hope you experience some version of this in your own life as well. But don't wait. Learn, build, serve and guide as best you can right now, as an everyday patriot making yourself available to your country and to your broader world, with your personal talents, your distinctive energy and your extraordinarily valuable time.

In one of the most famous battles of American history— the Alamo—at the end of a long time of nearly constant bombardment, things suddenly grew quiet. Colonel William Travis took out his sword and drew a line in the sand between himself and his remaining men. After explaining with great care the impossible situation they all faced at that moment, he said, "Those prepared to give their lives in freedom's cause, come over to me."

Instantly, all but one man stepped over the line. That lone individual remaining in place was the famous Jim Bowie, desperately sick with pneumonia and lying on a cot. He said, "Boys, carry me over," and that moment crossed into history.

★ ★ ★ ★ ★

The secret of man's being is not only to live
but to have something to live for.
Fyodor Dostoyevsky

★ ★ ★ ★ ★

I don't have a sword today, and I can't draw a line in the sand for you, wherever you are in your life. But I do have a request. If you are prepared to give your time, your attention, your actions and your sacred honor in freedom's cause, to keep this nation great and to keep alive the hope of the world for life, liberty and the pursuit of happiness, please cross the line of real, everyday patriotism, and make a commitment today to do something about it. Find out immediately how you can get more involved in your community, and then take action.

Remember the Alamo. And keep America great!

You can't do everything, but you have to do
Everything you can.
Horace

Appendix One: The Tools of Success

For many years, as a public philosopher, I've been bringing people the tools of success that have been identified for us over the centuries by the great thinkers who have gone before us. As I urge you to give your time and energy to projects that will benefit your community and our nation, I thought it would be important to list briefly the seven most universal conditions of success. They are developed at length in my books *True Success* (1994) and *The Art of Achievement* (2002), as well as in some of the essays on my website, www.MorrisInstitute.com. Come visit me online and use those essays to stimulate your own thoughts.

From the times of ancient philosophy on through to the present day, the wisest diagnosticians of the human condition have specified that, for true success in any worthy endeavor, we need The 7 Cs of Success:

(1) A clear **CONCEPTION** of what we want, a vivid vision, a goal clearly imagined.

(2) A strong **CONFIDENCE** that we can attain that goal.

(3) A focused **CONCENTRATION** on what it takes to reach the goal.

(4) A stubborn **CONSISTENCY** in pursuing our vision.

(5) An emotional **COMMITMENT** to the importance of what we're doing.

(6) A good **CHARACTER** to guide us and keep us on a proper course.

(7) A **CAPACITY TO ENJOY** the process along the way.

Without a use of these tools, without action in conformity with these simple but powerful conditions, the best possible intentions may never translate into the best possible results. With them, it's amazing what we can do.

Appendix Two: The Little Things

Everyday patriotism is based on one important insight: Little things can have big results. Don't overlook the small acts of citizenship and patriotic concern while dreaming of a better America for us all. You might:

Mentor someone at work.

Stand a little straighter during the National Anthem, sing a little louder, and convey to your kids the importance of this event.

When you see a policeman on duty, or security person in the airport, smile and say "Thanks for being here."

Coach or help out for a kids' soccer team or baseball league.

Volunteer to teach a Sunday School class at church. Or just go.

Attend a community meeting or town hall discussion of a pressing issue.

Shovel the snow off an elderly neighbor's drive, or, depending on your part of the country, offer to mow a lawn or haul away trash.

Find a way to give an hour or two a week to some volunteer work.

Read the Constitution to your kids at bedtime. Really.

Encourage your children to read a short, age appropriate book on the founding of our country.

Help in a political campaign, in however small a role.

Write a positive note to an elected official praising them on something you've seen them doing well.

When the local fire department has a fish fry or cookout for fund raising, go eat and have fun.

Write a constructive letter to the editor of your local paper on some issue or story you care about.

Read at least a book a year on the history or functioning of our country, and talk to someone about what you've read.

When you notice a problem, try to get involved in a solution.

★ ★ ★ ★ ★

The question in life is not "What can I get?"
but "What can I give?"
Robert Baden-Powell

★ ★ ★ ★ ★

Appendix Three: Places to Start

Here is a short list of sample organizations you can contact to see how you might be able to use your talents and time to make a positive difference for your community and our nation as a great everyday patriot.

More are listed at www.IndependenceRoadTrip.org.

The Boys and Girls Clubs

http://www.bgca.org

The Center for Voting and Democracy

http://www.fairvote.org

Close Up Foundation

http://www.closeup.org

The Content of Our character

http://www.contentofourcharacter.org

The Council for Excellence in Government

http://www.excelgov.org

Habitat for Humanity

http://www.habitat.org

Kids Voting USA

http://www.kidsvotingusa.org

The League of Women Voters
http://www.lwv.org

Rock the Vote
http://www.rockthevote.org

The United Way
http://national.unitedway.org

Youth Service America
http://www.ysa.org

Youth Vote Coalition
http://www.youthvote.org

Acknowledgements

I'd like to thank all the friends and colleagues who took time out of their busy schedules to read drafts of this little book whenever I needed a quick opinion, who encouraged me in its publication, and who contributed in various ways to its final form. Those who gave especially extensive attention to earlier stages of the book and provided helpful comments for its improvement were Dave Phillips, Neill Currie, Jerry Walls, Mim Harrison, Peter Osborne, Mary Yorke and my wife Mary Morris. I owe them a lot. This project could not have come into existence when it did without the commitment and assistance of master designer Dennis Walsak, whose work I admire and always appreciate.

I also want to thank all the great Americans I know who have inspired me to believe that in this amazing country the best is yet to come.

*****

No act of kindness, however small, is ever wasted.
Aesop

*****

About the Author

Tom Morris has become one of the most active business speakers and advisors in America due to his unusual ability to bring the greatest wisdom of the past into the challenges we face now. A native of North Carolina, Tom is a graduate of the University of North Carolina (Chapel Hill) and has been honored, along with Michael Jordan, as a recipient of its Distinguished Young Alumnus Award. He holds a Ph.D. in philosophy and religious studies from Yale University. For fifteen years he served as a professor of philosophy at the University of Notre Dame, where he quickly became one of the most popular teachers, in many years having as much as an eighth of the entire student body in his classes. He is now chairman of the Morris Institute for Human Values and can be reached through www.MorrisInstitute.com.

Tom's twelfth book, *True Success: A New Philosophy of Excellence*, launched him into a new adventure as a public philosopher and advisor to the corporate world. His audiences have included executives and leaders from such companies as General Motors, Ford Motor Company, Verizon, Unilever, IBM, Coca Cola, The US Air Force, International Paper, Price Waterhouse, Target Stores, Bayer, Deloitte and Touche, Federated Investors, Taco Bell, Minute Maid, the American Heart Association, and many of the largest national and international trade associations. He is also the author of the highly acclaimed book *If Aristotle Ran General Motors* and the even more recent *Philosophy for Dummies*. His fifteenth book, published in 2002, is *The Art of Achievement*.

Tom is the first philosopher in history to appear in network TV commercials, where he has served as the national spokesman on behalf of Disney Home Videos for Winnie the Pooh, a most philosophical bear.